Pearson
PUBLISHING

Student Handbook for Drama

Brian McGuire

Brian McGuire is a deputy headteacher and a drama practitioner.
He is recognised as one of the country's leading authorities on drama.
He has a great deal of experience as a senior examiner, keynote speaker
and leads national courses on drama for teachers.

Cartoons by Steve Clarke

(Based on original cartoons by Gary Hogg)

The author is grateful to the following students for some of the example
extracts which are based on their work: Katie Barrett, David Bracewell,
Clara Connelly, Zoe Dolen, Sarah Ellison, Hayley Fairclough, Laura Hart,
Kirsty Jolly, Debra Jones, John Smith, Leanne Stacey, Emma Stockton
and Cassia Wilson.

Hands off!

This book belongs to:
....

Name ....

Class ....

School ....

Date of exams...

Coursework deadline dates...

....

....

Exam board ....

Specification number ....

Candidate number...

Centre number ....

Further copies of this publication may be obtained from:

Pearson Publishing
Chesterton Mill, French's Road, Cambridge CB4 3NP
Tel 01223 350555 Fax 01223 356484
Email info@pearson.co.uk Web site www.pearsonpublishing.co.uk

ISBN: 1 85749 843 7 1

Published by Pearson Publishing 2003
© Pearson Publishing 2003
First published 1998
Second edition 2000
Third edition 2003

Contents

Introduction

Drama work generally covers three areas:

- improvisational work
- rehearsed presentations
- written responses.

The purpose of this handbook is to:

- introduce you to the drama process and its various parts. *Chapter 1* (pages 1 to 5) describes the drama process
- help you to understand how your sensitivity, creativity and communication skills are developed through drama. *Chapter 2* (pages 6 to 10) is devoted to these aspects of drama
- give you a clear understanding of the drama techniques used in improvisational drama. *Chapter 3* (pages 11 to 47) describes these drama techniques through the use of colourful cartoons. (Note that the term 'technique' is used throughout the book instead of 'convention'.)
- help you structure an improvisation ready for presentation. *Chapter 4* (pages 48 to 94) shows how you can develop your presentation step by step
- support and advise you on writing about your own drama work. *Chapter 5* (pages 95 to 120) contains many examples of written work; each example is discussed to show you why the work is effective and how it could be improved.

There are a number of forms in the handbook which you can use to make notes. In some cases, worked examples are included to show you how to use them.

With a better knowledge of the drama techniques you use, you will become more confident with the practical side of drama and should find it easier to evaluate your work in written form.

The benefits of studying drama

Studying drama develops skills that are important if your intention is to be involved with drama at some professional level, for example:

- performing arts courses
- acting
- stagecraft.

The study of drama will help you develop an appreciation of drama as an art form and its place in our society. Drama also makes an enormous contribution to your personal development. In today's world, employers are looking for mature, creative people who can communicate effectively – precisely the skills that drama develops.

Drama will help develop your ability to work as part of a team. It gives you the opportunity to understand different points of view, create your own opinions, listen purposefully and develop important language skills. It develops your sense of commitment and your ability to appreciate and appraise constructively. Drama encourages planning and research techniques, and physical and perceptual skills.

The content of your lessons will help you to understand the values, issues and culture of today's world.

In brief, it develops your:

- sensitivity
- creativity
- communication skills.

And it is a subject you will enjoy!

The *Technical Companion to Drama* is also available from Pearson Publishing. Visit our Web site at www.pearsonpublishing.co.uk for more drama-related titles.

1 The drama process

The drama process can be broken down into three main parts:

- the content
- the drama skills and techniques
- the personal and social skills.

The content of the drama

Some teachers refer to the content as the topic, issue or project. For example, the content could be ageism, sexism, crime, happiness or loneliness. Alternatively, the content can be more specific. For example, through drama you could look at the story of a miner, a wedding, or the relationship between a mother and her son. You might meet the content through improvisation work or through a text. A text could be a:

- script, extract or full play
- poem or song
- newspaper or magazine article
- letter or prose.

Your teacher may use other sources for the content, for example, a painting, a photograph or an object.

There may be a particular issue in the content that you or your teacher wish to pursue more than others or you may wish to pursue a number of issues. *Romeo and Juliet* is the story of two lovers but the play is also about family feuding, friendship, loyalty, etc.

If you are looking at a topic on loneliness, you might consider the loneliness of an old person, how someone young can be lonely, how someone can be lonely in a crowd, or possible consequences of loneliness. By role-playing situations that show an old person and a young person as lonely, you may conclude that, in many cases, a young person's loneliness is temporary and an old person's loneliness may be more permanent.

The content in the drama lesson could aim to:
- give you the opportunity to make sense of topical issues
- look at information or a particular point of view on a topic
- relate information to your point of view
- help you adjust your point of view
- develop ideas.

Alternatively, it may be to do with specific learning such as facts about a topic, eg The Jarrow March took place in 1936.

Drama content can link across subjects and your teacher may set up cross-curricular projects (ie Drama working with another subject). For example, immigration and open-cast mining could link with Geography; world wars could link with History; and the study of Shakespeare, specific poems and themes from novels link with English.

The content is only one part of the drama process but it is the content that will drive the drama. It will give it credibility and purpose.

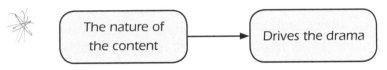

The nature of the content → Drives the drama

Drama skills and techniques

In order to look at the content, your drama teacher will use a variety of drama skills and techniques. For example, in a role-play you may improvise a situation with a partner, a small group or the whole class. With a partner, one of you may play the part of the parent or guardian and the other a teenager asking for more pocket money. Role-plays can be as simple as this example but may be more complicated such as when you use the 'mantle of the expert' technique. This is where you take on the role of someone who is an expert in a particular field, for example, students in the class might be police inspectors trying to solve a crime.

There are many other drama techniques such as thought tunnel, thought in the head, freeze-frame, etc. *Chapter 3* offers detailed explanations of drama techniques (see pages 11 to 47). Hopefully, the cartoons will help you to remember the definitions.

The drama skills and techniques make the drama form, in other words the shape of the work.

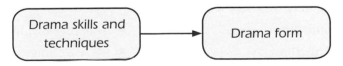

Drama skills and techniques → Drama form

Your drama teacher will:

- introduce you to different drama forms
- find appropriate drama forms for you to work with
- create opportunities for you to participate in and view drama
- help you to make progress with your ability to select and use drama skills and techniques.

Personal and social skills

In order for the drama work to be successful, personal and social skills play an important part – skills such as concentration, organising others, working together, making decisions, listening and planning. Many of these personal and social skills are happening as a matter of course in a drama lesson but there is the opportunity for your drama teacher to emphasise particular skills. For example, your drama teacher can set up situations within the drama that allow all students to contribute to the ideas or create opportunities of leadership for those who do not normally lead. Drama develops many personal and social skills, including:

- Leading a team
- Organising others
- Understanding and speaking in different registers
- Developing language skills
- Putting across a point of view
- Concentration
- Sharing
- Motivating
- Being supportive
- Courteousness
- Appreciating
- Reliability
- Being able to select materials
- Structuring
- Resourcefulness
- Shaping ideas
- Realising ideas
- Contributing
- Being organised
- Listening
- Perseverance
- Appraising
- Confidence
- Purposefulness
- Creating opinion
- Assertiveness
- Enthusiasm
- Being flexible
- Being considerate
- Cooperation
- Planning
- Meeting deadlines
- Researching
- Sustaining ideas

Each part of the drama process (ie content, drama skills and techniques, personal and social skills) offers specific learning opportunities. The power in drama is when all three parts come together.

The drama process

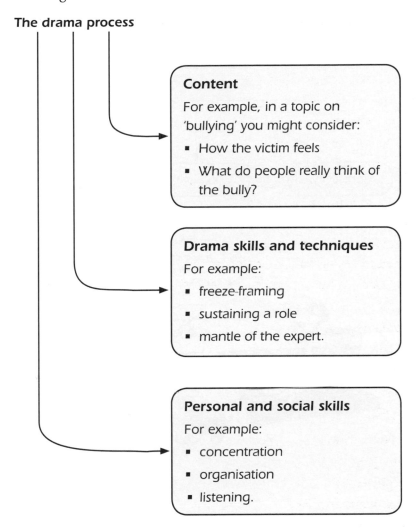

Content

For example, in a topic on 'bullying' you might consider:

- How the victim feels
- What do people really think of the bully?

Drama skills and techniques

For example:

- freeze-framing
- sustaining a role
- mantle of the expert.

Personal and social skills

For example:

- concentration
- organisation
- listening.

When in role, or when watching the drama, you may become emotionally involved. In other words, you care about the characters and the situations. Sometimes when people watch a play, they laugh, they cry or worry about the characters. This is the aesthetic – the emotional living out of the drama. This is what makes drama special – the process involves the emotions. To the content of the drama you bring your own experiences. The drama work may help you consider your point of view on a topic and it develops your sensitivity.

2 Developing sensitivity, creativity and communication skills through drama

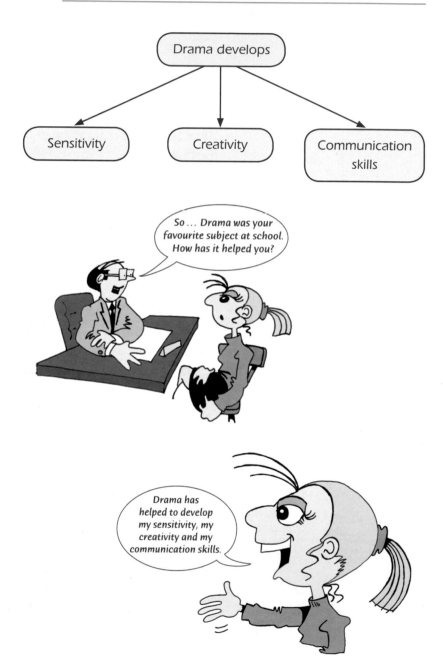

Drama develops

Sensitivity

Creativity

Communication skills

So ... Drama was your favourite subject at school. How has it helped you?

Drama has helped to develop my sensitivity, my creativity and my communication skills.

Sensitivity

The development of sensitivity through drama takes place when you watch or participate. You react to the areas of:

- content
- drama skills and techniques
- personal and social skills.

You can be sensitive to each area.

Being sensitive to content

The content can evoke emotion. If you read a poem or script about a person who is lonely, you react to its sense, in other words what it is about. You can feel sorry for the person. When you watch theatre, you react to the story and the way in which the characters appear to think.

Being sensitive to drama skills and techniques

You appreciate the shape of the drama, the use of form or how a skill is used. You may be watching the most earth-shattering moment in a play but all you are thinking is, 'Yes, I like the use of the red light on that area'. You watch your friends present a short improvisation and it finishes with a freeze-frame or a sound collage and you enjoy and admire the piece of drama because of the way in which they ended it. When you participate in a role-play, you try to use the right sort of language. You try to speak in a way that you think someone would in a particular situation. When you take on the role of an adult, you speak differently to the way you would speak when role-playing a five-year-old. The drama form we choose can make the experience more intensive. Adding music, for example, can evoke a very emotional response.

Being sensitive to personal and social skills

Commitment is one of the most important personal and social skills related to the drama process. If you do not commit to the role-play then it does not work. When you observe a play, you admire the fact that the actor has practised to perfect the presentation; you appreciate their hard work; you admire the confidence of someone as they perform.

You can react to content, drama skills and personal and social skills separately or to a combination of two or three of them. When you watch drama and react to all three at once then the sensation is stronger and more intense. When participating in drama, the trick is to get the right balance. When an actor is performing, they can become carried away by the content and can lose control of the drama form. They can become so affected by the meaning of the words that they lose control of their voice.

Creativity

Being creative with content

In the area of content, you respond creatively to the ideas the drama evokes. You then develop those ideas, often seeing them through to presentation.

Being creative with drama skills and techniques

You explore the structure and shape of the drama. Sometimes you may experiment and play with the form or structure and this can actually move the ideas forward. You might decide to add a freeze-frame at the end. Alternatively, you may decide to add some slow motion or mime. When participating in a drama and creating a presentation, you manipulate, change and adapt the drama form.

Being creative with personal and social skills

Through personal and social skills, drama helps you to develop a creative way of working together. This is through leading and collaborating with people. There may be instances when you are trying to persuade other students in your group to present the drama in a way that you believe to be effective. There may be someone who does not want to join in so you devise ways of helping them to be part of the drama. When we are dealing with people, we devise ways of motivating them and ways for us to work together. Drama is very much about working together.

Communication

Communication skills and content

Issues may be raised by the content of the drama. You can communicate these issues and your ideas to other students in your group, your teacher or the class.

Communication skills and drama skills and techniques

The communication of your ideas can be through the drama form, ie this can be done through your role-play or a prepared improvisation.

Communication skills and personal and social skills

Drama offers you the opportunity to develop ways of creating effective communication with other people in your group or class. If you shout when organising a group, they may not want to accept your idea. The way in which you speak to people influences how they react to you. Drama helps you to become an effective communicator. Through drama, students can develop their language skills.

So along with content, drama skills and techniques and personal and social skills, we have sensitivity, creativity and communication skills. The table on the following page summarises the links between the drama process and the development of sensitivity, creativity and communication skills.

The drama process

	Sensitivity	Creativity	Communication
Content	Sensitivity towards the issues raised by the drama	Creative thinking in response to: • the drama content • developing ideas • seeing ideas through	Communicating ideas raised by the drama content
Drama skills and techniques	• Using and selecting appropriate drama form in a sensitive way • Appreciation of drama form	Creative thinking in relation to the use of drama form	Communicating ideas through use of the drama form
Personal and social skills	• Working as a team member and/or leading • Responding in a sensitive way to others in the team • Appreciation of the personal and social skills of others	Developing creative ways of leading and collaborating	• Communicating with others involved in the drama work • Developing language skills

3 Drama techniques

The drama techniques make the drama form. This is the way of presenting the drama work that you or your teacher chooses. As you become familiar with the techniques, you will be able to use them to explore or enhance your own work. The various techniques provide tools to develop ideas, characters and plots. They build the drama and help you to understand the content and issues raised. It is important to have a good understanding of the techniques when writing about your drama work.

The techniques can be broken down into three main areas:
- Basic role-play techniques (pages 12 to 20)
- Basic improvisation techniques (pages 21 to 31)
- Presentation skills (pages 32 to 43).

Most of the definitions are accompanied by a cartoon to help you to remember the technique. A checklist is provided on page 44 so that you can keep a record of the techniques you have used.

Basic role-play techniques

Role-play

 Using your own values and attitudes, you place yourself in an imagined situation.

For example, you may be a scientist on an expedition in South America. The role-play may be about the meeting of all the people who are going on the expedition. This role-play probably involves the whole group at once.

Role-plays can also take place in pairs or small groups. In pair work or small group work, your teacher may ask you to find an area in which to work. All the role-plays will begin together. An example of pair work might be where one student plays the role of a parent or guardian and the other a teenager who has come home late. The role-play begins with the teenager trying to creep into the house. After the teacher's instructions, all the role-plays commence together. They finish when the teacher feels the role-plays are over.

Role-plays are not watched by an audience.

Preparing for the role

Sometimes your drama teacher may want you to prepare for the role. You will have to decide on background information.

For example, when in role as an old person, you may invent family background and past events. Teachers often use exercises to help you. For example, freeze-framing an aspect from the old person's life, hotseating or interviewing. If a lot of preparation goes on, then it is likely that your teacher will expect the role you are playing to last a reasonable amount of time. They will expect you to be able to sustain and develop the role.

Sustaining the role

Keeping the role going, not dropping out of role.

It is sometimes difficult to concentrate on staying in role. However, the more role-plays you take part in, the easier you will find it. At first the role-plays may be short but, as you become more used to drama, the role-plays will last longer.

Developing the role

Over a period of time and as the drama continues you build up the role.

Sometimes the role can be taken over by someone else in the group. This may give you other points of view the character might have and can also give you the opportunity to see further ideas as to how the role can develop.

Language of the role

When in role you adopt the correct oral and body language.

Adults speak in a different way to children. Politicians have a particular way of speaking. Often getting the language right means including particular words that the person would use. Think about how people greet each other. Consider the way two 11-year-olds would greet each other. Compare this to the way two business people would greet each other: the business people would probably shake hands; the two 11-year-olds would not. The language of the business people would probably be more formal, for example, 'Good afternoon. I'm pleased to see you'. The language of the two 11-year-olds would probably be more informal, for example, 'Hiya!'.

Role-reversal

This is where you swap roles with another student so that you can see both points of view.

For instance, one student plays the boss, the other the employee being sacked. Later in the drama they swap roles. This is often done with simple pair role-play.

Role within a role

You adopt a role in a particular situation. Your character then has to role-play some situation within the drama.

For example, if your class were playing a group of business people on a training course, you may be asked to present a mock interview. In this case, you would be playing a business person playing an interviewee.

Writing in role

When in role, you create written work.

This might be in the form of a letter or a diary extract. For example, as a soldier in the trench, you could complete a postcard to be sent home from the war zone. As a villager, you could complain about the proposed open-cast mine by writing a letter to the local council.

Writing in role helps you to deepen your understanding of the events of the drama. A piece of writing in role can be useful to include in GCSE Drama written work. Remember that it will need some analysis or comments to go with it to place it in context within the drama.

Secret role-play

Also called hidden role-play and special information. The teacher gives information to some students but not others.

For example, in pair role-play, the teacher may say to one student that they have been in trouble for stealing. Acting as a parent or guardian in the role-play, the partner attempts to find out information. In ensemble role-play, a student or a group of students are given special information. For example, as town planners they are presenting a project to the local community (the rest of the class in role). The teacher has given the town planners particular information about the project.

Role-on-the-wall

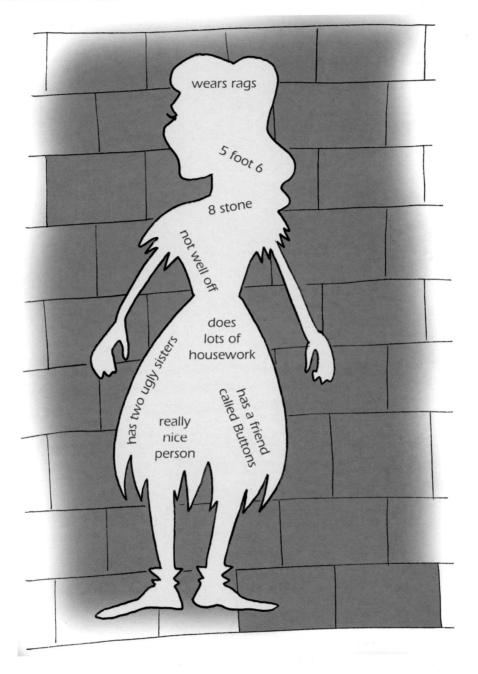

wears rags

5 foot 6

8 stone

not well off

has two ugly sisters

does lots of housework

has a friend called Buttons

really nice person

Method 1: Your drama teacher draws an outline of a human figure on a large piece of paper. Details about the central character of the role-play are written inside the outline by the teacher and the group.

This builds up a picture of the central role in the drama. Information about the character's education can be written in the right arm, hobbies in the left, family background in the head and so on. Information about how others see the character or particular pressures on the character can be written outside the outline.

There is a number of possible areas of information to write up. You can choose from the following or make up your own titles:

- Personal details

- Wealth

- Health

- Job

- Loves and hates

- Ambitions

- Places of importance

- Concerns and worries

- Secrets

- People admired

- Recent past

- Important childhood events

- Relatives

- Education

- Intelligence

- Habitat

- Important items owned

- Something the person is proud of or ashamed of

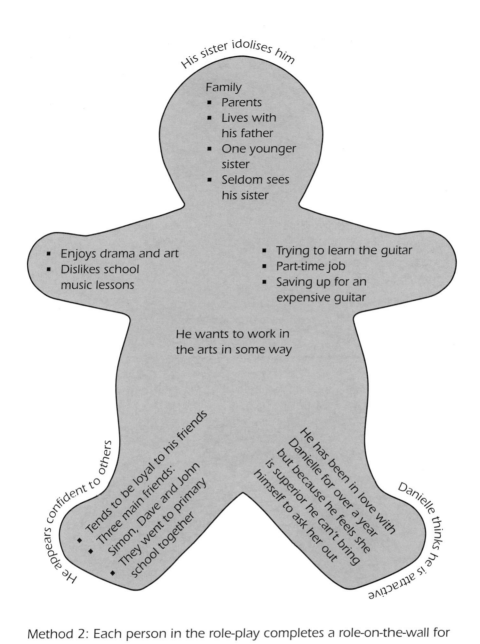

His sister idolises him

Family
- Parents
- Lives with his father
- One younger sister
- Seldom sees his sister

- Enjoys drama and art
- Dislikes school music lessons

- Trying to learn the guitar
- Part-time job
- Saving up for an expensive guitar

He wants to work in the arts in some way

He appears confident to others

Tends to be loyal to his friends
- Three main friends: Simon, Dave and John
- They went to primary school together

He has been in love with Danielle for over a year but because he feels she is superior he can't bring himself to ask her out

Danielle thinks he is attractive

He is attractive

Method 2: Each person in the role-play completes a role-on-the-wall for their role.

This is a useful device when you are working on a prepared piece of drama, particularly for a final GCSE Drama presentation. It helps you develop credibility for your character. You can help each other with your role-on-the-wall.

Mantle of the expert

In the role-play, the group take on roles as experts.

For example, a group of detectives involved in a particular case, a group of doctors, a group of architects or designers. Generally, there will be a problem that needs solving. Mantle of the expert is a popular way of involving the whole class at once. Your teacher may give you information or ask you to complete some research about the role.

Teacher in role

Here your teacher takes part in the role-play.

Your teacher could be the leader of an expedition, for example. Alternatively, they may take a less forceful role. For example, as a messenger or the assistant to the director of a company.

If you are role-playing in small groups, your teacher may join in by taking on a role. This gives the teacher the opportunity to ask questions of your role, thereby allowing you to consider issues related to the drama.

Basic improvisation techniques

Freeze-frame

The creation of a still image. The action is frozen like a photograph.

Freeze-frames can focus on some part of the role-play or improvisation. At other times, the freeze-frame can be carefully built and can be the starting point for the drama. Sometimes your teacher may ask you or your group to build up the freeze frame using one person at a time. The teacher could ask you to bring the freeze-frame to life, ie go straight into a role-play. At other times, the teacher may ask you to speak the thoughts of the character in the freeze-frame.

You may be asked to create a series of freeze-frames to give the outline of a story. When asked to do this, you should move from one frame to another with the minimum of fuss. Melting one freeze-frame into another (ie changing one freeze-frame to another in a slow, deliberate and controlled way) helps develop an awareness of space, movement and links.

When you make a freeze-frame, always choose a stance you can control so that you can keep still. When you present a freeze-frame, you need to consider blocking in and you should try to make the freeze-frame visually interesting.

Bringing to life

In groups, students make a freeze-frame. The teacher tells you to bring the frame to life. The students role-play until the teacher calls 'Freeze'.

Spotlighting

During the role-play(s), the teacher asks everyone to stop apart from one person, a couple or a small group who continue with the role-play. Everyone else observes.

Your teacher may decide to start the role-play(s) again. Spotlighting could take place several times.

Focus in

Selecting a brief extract from one part of the role-play or improvisation.

Generally, the focus in is presented to others. The focus may only be on a freeze-frame or 15 seconds of the drama. The focus could be on a particularly important moment from the drama. For example, if the role-play is about a teenager leaving home, the focus might be 15 seconds before they walk out of the door.

Marking the moment

You choose a moment from the role-play that you feel was pertinent to you. A moment when perhaps you felt you understood the issue. A significant moment from the drama.

It can be presented through a freeze-frame or very brief improvisation.

Hotseating

 In role and without any preparation you answer questions about yourself.

The questions can be asked by the teacher or other students. Sometimes the teacher adopts a role and takes the hotseat. Hotseating helps build up information about a role. It helps the person in role create opinions and points of view.

Interviewing

This is where two students are in role. One of you plays the interviewee, the other the interviewer.

For example, you might play a reporter interviewing a king. In another example, the interviewer might be a doctor or a detective trying to find out particular information. There can be more than one interviewee or interviewer. This technique is a little bit like hotseating except all participants are in role.

Thought in the head

When the role-play is frozen or a freeze frame is made, you speak the thought in the character's head.

This helps develop the role and gives you the chance to hear the thoughts of other characters in the drama. It is also known as thought tracking. Sometimes you might want to present a brief scene with the thoughts in a character's head being said by another student.

Thought tunnel

A character from the drama walks slowly between two rows of students. As the character passes each student, they call out what they think the character is thinking.

For example, a person is being bullied at school. Someone takes on this role. As they walk down the thought tunnel, other students call out their thoughts, for example:

- 'I wonder what will happen today?'

- 'Should I go to school?'

- 'Should I report the bullying?'

For a character in a dilemma, one side of the tunnel could put one viewpoint and the other side can take the opposing view. The thought tunnel is also known as conscience alley or thought pathway.

Giving witness/ making point of view

In role, you describe some event you have witnessed, giving the details from your point of view.

For example, you may have witnessed a robbery, an accident or a parade. This is a useful technique to use in historical dramas, eg you could describe the time you saw the first car, a public hanging, a workhouse or a coronation.

Good angel/bad angel

This technique is generally used in groups of three. To the left, one person plays the good angel, and to the right, another person plays the bad angel. The central character could be in some sort of dilemma; there is a decision to be made. Through the good and bad angels, they can consider different points of view.

For example, should he truant with his friends or go to school? The person playing the good angel gives reasons why he should not truant, and the person playing the bad angel gives reasons why he should truant. This is a useful technique to use with classroom or studio work but can also be effective in prepared improvisations. For dramatic effect, more than one good and bad angel can be used.

His/her thoughts

A person acts out a particular situation. Their partner or a small group relates the thoughts that person might be having.

For example, a mother is leaving a baby in a bus shelter. The partner relates the mother's thoughts to the audience during the action.

Sometimes the central person may not be involved in any direct action but may simply sit, stand or hold a freeze-frame. This technique is useful in prepared improvisations and will often be used by your teacher in improvisation work.

Re-enactment

An event that you have been made aware of through the drama is re-enacted.

This is done through role-play or prepared improvisation. For example, if the drama is looking at why a person has ended up in prison then some scenes from the prisoner's childhood might be enacted.

Forum theatre

Some students role-play a scene from the drama. The others in the group or class observe the role-play. The group watching can enter the scene as any character or they can stop a scene and take over a role.

For example, if the group is watching a drama about a young girl discussing her pregnancy with her mother, members of the group could join in as the father, boyfriend or sister. If you wish to take over one of the roles, you raise your hand and the teacher stops the drama by calling 'Freeze'. You then take over the role from the other player who then joins the forum (audience). When the drama is stopped, you and the rest of the group can comment or make suggestions on the characters' reactions to the dramatic situation.

How close?

A character from the drama stands or sits in the centre of the room. The other students take up positions of distance or closeness to that person. The distance represents the relationship between the characters.

For example, the doctor stands in the centre. Near him is the patient whose life he has just saved. Near the patient is the patient's family. Further away are the administrators of the hospital.

Often in this exercise your teacher will ask for your thought in the head (see page 25).

Framing

Your teacher puts the drama into a context by helping you choose the direction in which the drama can go.

You may choose the context or issue. For example, the issue may concern a girl who is leaving home. You may show through improvisation or suggestions why the girl wants to leave home. The reasons may be different from group to group. Your teacher helps you to choose one reason. Thus, the first part of the drama is framed. You may then look at incidents in the girl's life during her first week away from home. Again, your teacher and the group decide on which incidents you feel are appropriate to your drama. Thus, the next part of the drama is framed.

Your teacher may suggest which drama form is to be used. For example, if the drama is about villagers who are opposed to a bypass, the teacher may suggest that each of you decides on a role in the village. You might show three freeze-frames from your everyday life and one short scene of how the bypass might affect you. After these exercises, the teacher may suggest that in role you attend a meeting about the bypass at the town hall.

Caption making

You devise a phrase or sentence that suggests what the drama is about.

The caption can fit a freeze-frame or piece of drama. For example, if the drama is about an employer sacking an employee, the title might be 'No longer required'.

Fixing space

You use the furniture or rostra or acknowledge boundary lines for your role-play or improvisation.

Fixing space is where you create your own functional set or space in which to work.

Solo thinking

Students sit on the floor in a space by themselves. The teacher asks them to consider an issue or a particular role.

The teacher may give some ideas or key questions for the students to consider. After a while, the teacher may ask the students some direct questions or ask them to take on a role and share some of the thoughts the person might be having (thought in the head).

Sometimes after solo thinking, the teacher may suggest that each student makes a different statement about a character from the drama. These statements build up information on the character. Solo thinking is often used by the drama teacher at the end of a lesson so that the students are given the opportunity to consider the issues raised and the learning points of the session.

Presentation skills

Thinking time

Time given to you before the role-play starts. You consider the information given about the role and think about how you will act in the role-play.

Improvisation/ prepared improvisation

Make up and act out a storyline with little preparation. For a prepared improvisation you are given time for rehearsal.

The prepared improvisation is presented to an audience, generally the rest of the class.

Workshop presentation

In workshop presentations the prepared improvisations are presented to an audience outside of the drama group.

For example, a Year 10 GCSE Drama group presents prepared improvisations on the theme of bullying to Year 7, or a Year 9 class presents work to primary school pupils on the theme of starting a new school. The workshop could include some interaction with the performance work. The visitors may be able to join in (like forum theatre) or may be given some specific follow-up tasks which may include drama work.

Mime

A storyline is acted out through movement and gesture without the character speaking.

Characters do not mouth words. The movement and gestures make clear the drama. Often in improvisation work there are no properties (eg glasses or cups), so you will have to mime actions such as taking a drink or eating a meal. These situations can be difficult, as you have to concentrate on your reactions to another character and the mime of holding the glass. If you forget that you are supposed to be holding a glass, this can create an unwanted comical effect.

Sequencing

In all prepared drama work there needs to be some sort of order. The storyline needs to be in a logical sequence.

You decide upon the order of events or scenes.

Voice patterns

This is how you use your voice to create the right tone for the role.

You may need to shout to show anger or whisper to show fear. You need to consider the rhythm, pace and intonation of your voice. For example:

- How quickly or slowly will the character speak?

- Which words would they stress?

Intonation is when the voice goes up or down thus adding expression to the words.

When speaking in performance always listen to yourself. It will help slow you down and help with clarity (how clear you are). If it sounds right to you, you are probably speaking too fast.

Remember that an audience only gets the opportunity to hear a line once. It is also important to speak with more volume than normal as your voice has to travel to reach the audience.

Addressing the audience

In the presentation of a prepared improvisation, one or more of the characters speak directly to the audience.

Generally the rest of the action is frozen whilst this occurs. This allows the character to comment on events of the drama or give further information to the audience. It is a little like the role of narrator, but the person(s) addressing the audience has a role in the story.

Narrating

In the presentation of a drama piece, one or more actors speak directly to the audience, giving information and relating events of the story.

Often, the narrator will not be a character in the story. The narrative of the drama is the storyline.

Soliloquy

In role, you speak to the audience.

You share your thoughts, thus giving the audience further insight into your character and events.

Dramatic pause

During the dialogue a short silence is created.

A dramatic pause in the dialogue can help build up the tension. Sometimes in presentation work, the silences can be just as effective as the words spoken. Remember, however, that if you use too many silences they can lose their effect.

Blocking in

This is the position someone takes in relation to the acting area and the audience.

The blocking in is to allow for sightlines, ie characters are placed on the stage or acting area so that the audience can see them clearly. When presenting improvisations, always block in the actors downstage. It makes it easier for the audience to see and hear.

The blocking in of a character can also be symbolic. For example, the king can be placed on a higher level than the servant.

Facing out of the drama

In prepared improvisations, anyone from the performing group not involved with the immediate action of the drama stands and faces upstage.

With their backs to the audience, this signifies they are not involved. This helps cut down on stage traffic. Stage traffic is the movement of actors as they continually enter and exit. Facing out of the drama helps to make the piece seem less disjointed and cuts down on the number of blackouts between scenes.

Turning through the audience

When turning to face another actor in the acting area, try to make the turn bigger by turning through the longest way.

For example, actor A, who is facing upstage, has to turn to actor B:

Actor A *Actor B*

Actor A should turn through 270° by:

1   turning away from actor B so that his left shoulder is downstage

2   then facing directly downstage

3   turning to actor B so that his right shoulder is downstage.

The three stages are all one continuous action. It allows the audience to see more of the actor's face as he turns. This is useful if it is important for the audience to be aware of a character's thoughts as they turn.

Slow motion

During part of a presented improvisation, the action is deliberately slowed. Often this is used to focus on a particular part of the improvisation.

Sometimes scenes showing events such as fights or races are shown in slow motion for greater visual impact.

Symbolism

Symbolism is the use of abstract form – using gestures, movement or words to represent the content of the drama.

When a piece is symbolic or abstract it does not look realistic. For example, if we want to symbolise pressure on teenagers, we might stand one person centre stage. The other students from the group might stand on higher levels and point at the teenager. Each person may repeat one or two words to represent pressure. One person might say 'No money', someone else 'Girlfriend', another 'Work', and so on. As the words are repeated, they become like a chant. The teenager eventually curls up into a ball.

Sound collage

In sound collage, different sounds are created with voice or instruments that overlap to make a dramatic effect.

Sound collage is a useful way of creating variations in the sounds that the audience hears. For example, the sounds created by the

actors surrounding the man taking his driving test symbolise different sounds that may be going round in his head. The repetition of the sounds helps to create for the audience the confusion and stress that the driver feels. The example given in the definition of symbolism also shows the use of sound collage.

Amplifying

Sometimes called 'more and more'. The drama can be presented using abstract or realistic form. The dialogue or voice patterns begin very quietly and become louder and louder, or the actions begin very small and become bigger and bigger.

Of course, both the actions and the dialogue or voice patterns can increase at the same time.

Split staging

The acting area is split into two, or sometimes more, areas.

In area A, the actors hold a freeze. The actors in area B present action from the drama. After a while, the actors in area B freeze and the actors in area A bring their drama to life. The action can move between area A and area B several times. The drama will look better if the freeze-frames are visually interesting.

Docudrama

Students present a piece of drama in the style of a TV documentary.

The documentary may contain various interviews, action apparently caught on camera, re-enactments, reporters, link presenters, etc. It is often fun to present a docudrama of a character from literature, eg Macbeth. The docudrama could show interviews with the witches, Lady Macbeth or castle servants. Perhaps the police could be involved!

In the round

In the drama lesson, improvisations are performed with the class sitting round the edge of the acting area.

This comes from theatre in the round, when the audience sits all around the acting area. Often the class makes a circle with their chairs.

Drama techniques checklist

You should now understand the following terms. Tick the boxes to show which ones you have used in your drama lessons:

Basic role-play techniques

- ☐ Role-play
- ☐ Preparing for the role
- ☐ Sustaining the role
- ☐ Developing the role
- ☐ Language of the role
- ☐ Role-reversal
- ☐ Role within a role
- ☐ Writing in role
- ☐ Secret role-play
- ☐ Role-on-the-wall
- ☐ Mantle of the expert
- ☐ Teacher in role

Basic improvisation techniques

- ☐ Freeze-frame
- ☐ Bringing to life
- ☐ Spotlighting
- ☐ Focus in
- ☐ Marking the moment
- ☐ Hotseating
- ☐ Interviewing
- ☐ Thought in the head
- ☐ Thought tunnel
- ☐ Giving witness/ making point of view
- ☐ Good angel/bad angel
- ☐ His/her thoughts
- ☐ Re-enactment
- ☐ Forum theatre

- ☐ How close?
- ☐ Framing
- ☐ Caption making
- ☐ Fixing space
- ☐ Solo thinking

Presentation skills

- ☐ Thinking time
- ☐ Improvisation/ prepared improvisation
- ☐ Workshop presentation
- ☐ Mime
- ☐ Sequencing
- ☐ Voice patterns
- ☐ Addressing the audience
- ☐ Narrating
- ☐ Soliloquy
- ☐ Dramatic pause
- ☐ Blocking in
- ☐ Facing out of the drama
- ☐ Turning through the audience
- ☐ Slow motion
- ☐ Symbolism
- ☐ Sound collage
- ☐ Split staging
- ☐ Docudrama
- ☐ In the round

Expectations at Key Stage 3

By the end of year 7 you will have covered basic drama skills and techniques and will be aware of how the drama process works. You should be able to identify and talk about some of the techniques and skills, identify and understand the issues that go with the drama and be aware of the contribution that personal and social skills make to the drama process.

Year 8 will reinforce the basic drama skills and techniques. You should be able to develop them as well as adding new ones. Your skills of organisation, listening and sensitivity towards the drama should have improved.

Year 9 will further reinforce basic drama skills and techniques, and introduce you to more advanced skills and techniques. You should be able to select appropriate form (including abstract), as well as appraise in written and oral form with supportive evidence. You should be able to contribute effectively, working well with all types and sizes of groups.

Your drama teacher may award you a level. Their judgement will be based on criteria such as:

Level 4
- Can make some sense of the issue.
- Can create and sustain simple role-play.
- Can work in different sized groups.
- Can contribute some ideas.
- Shows some understanding of the basic performing conventions, eg simple blocking in for sightlines, supporting others in role.

Level 5

- Can sequence events effectively.
- Mostly makes a contribution and maintains concentration.
- Has an understanding of role-play in relation to pair, group and ensemble work.
- Can develop a role.
- Has a reasonable understanding of basic performing conventions and can attempt some experimentation with drama form.
- Can use abstract form with guidance.
- Can work in different sized and mixed gender groups.

Level 6

- Can select appropriate conventions, including abstract form.
- Can distinguish quality of performance.
- Shows a good understanding of the issues raised.
- Has awareness of interpretation.
- Can create and sustain roles with imagination.
- Makes a worthwhile contribution to the drama work.

Level 7

- Has good oral evaluation with ability to give evidence to support.
- Can select and experiment with different drama forms (including abstract).
- Can create and sustain thoughtful, credible roles.
- Makes a consistent contribution to the drama work, initiating ideas as well as listening to others.
- Has perceptive imagination in relation to space and movement.

Level 8

- Can develop drama with sensitivity using a wide range of drama techniques and skills.
- Has very good oral and written evaluation skills with ability to call on supportive evidence.
- Leads, organises and listens carefully to others.
- Can create and sustain complex roles.
- Has an awareness of how to use space and movement purposefully.

Exceptional level

- An excellent awareness of performance elements.
- Can recognise and use symbolism or abstract form effectively.
- An excellent understanding of role in relation to the drama.
- Can adopt a variety of roles with excellent understanding of appropriate language.
- A sustained and sensitive approach to all aspects of the drama process.
- Can evaluate very effectively, orally, in written form and with supportive evidence from all parts of the drama process.

A student will have achieved all the criteria in the levels below their allocated level.

4 Developing an improvisation

This chapter is intended to help you to prepare an improvisation for performance or an examination.

Developing an improvisation for presentation is a popular part of drama lessons. Taking an idea and developing it into a dramatic piece ready to perform for an audience can give a great deal of satisfaction. When preparing the improvisation, you need to look at how you can structure the development process. Simply repeating the play or improvisation over and over again will not necessarily improve it. You need to use ways of exploring the plot and characters so that they are credible and interesting to the audience. You need to know how to develop specific areas of performance, for example:

- vocal quality (how to use your voice)
- presenting a role (its credibility and interest)
- use of space and movement
- performance elements (pace, linking of scenes, highlights, etc).

(Pages 67 to 69 draw particular attention to these areas and consider what a drama examiner looks for.)

This chapter gives ideas for developing character and plot. For example, under the part on shaping and character development (page 54) it suggests switching roles or creating a re-enactment. These techniques help create more information about characters and could even be used as an extra scene. The methods suggested are not new. They are the tools or techniques you use during drama lessons. Normally, your teacher decides what techniques will be used in a lesson, but when developing your improvisation you can choose the techniques you think will help to move the drama on. These techniques are illustrated in *Chapter 3* (pages 11 to 43).

This chapter also contains tips on general performance elements, such as the number of scenes, blocking, etc. There are also notes on the final rehearsals and presentation. The chapter begins with advice on selecting a theme and getting the improvisation started. There are brief references to the design work of lighting, sound and set design. However, this book does not go into detail in these areas. (The *Technical Companion to Drama*, Pearson Publishing, offers useful notes on these areas.)

As you develop a presentation, you will go through the following process:

1 **Selecting a theme** – This will be done by you or with the help of your teacher.

2 **Exploring a theme** – Try out some ideas. Your teacher may create some drama lessons which allow you to explore a number of aspects of the theme before you decide on the precise nature of the improvisation. This work can often take place before groups are chosen.

3 **Choosing a group**

4 **Making sure you are aware of the examination requirements**

5 **Focus and title** – Once you focus on a theme you are going to follow, try to complete the focus boxes as soon as possible (see pages 53 and 72).

6 **Initial development of context** – Once the process has begun, you need to map out a general outline for the piece.

7 **Shaping and character development**

8 **Developing the structure** – Ask yourself the following:
   - Will it keep the interest of the audience all the way through?
   - Are there particular moments of interest?
   - Are there enough or too many scenes?

9 **Developing the performance elements**, ie:
   - Voice
   - Costumes and props
   - Music
   - Sets
   - Lighting
   - Blocking in
   - Levels

10 **Preparing and organising technical rehearsals**

11 **Preparing and organising the final rehearsal**

12 **Presenting the piece**

13 **Evaluating the piece**

Selecting a theme

Your teacher may give you a theme, or you could be asked to choose your own. There are a number of ways you can select a theme:

Topics already covered

You may like to revisit a theme completed earlier in the course or at Key Stage 3.

Topics derived from stimuli

This is a way of working often used by drama teachers. You could base an improvisation on:

- a newspaper article
- a picture or photograph
- a poem or piece of narrative
- an object
- proverbs, stories or other texts.

Often by using an object, the idea of symbolism can be introduced to the narrative. For example, a cup could belong to someone. It may be very special to them. It may symbolise a particular part of their life. When that part of their life becomes unimportant, the cup is destroyed. What could the following symbolise?

- A feather
- A pen
- A book
- A shell
- A chair

Text adaptations

You may wish to present extracts or interpretations from the storyline of a well-known text. Explore the theme, maybe putting the characters in different, modern or futuristic situations. How many times has *Romeo and Juliet* been interpreted? Perhaps consider a modern version of *Macbeth*, for example:

> In 2003, Macbeth and his friend Banquo visit Blackpool. They decide to visit a fortune teller. The fortune teller makes three predictions to Macbeth.

Place

By selecting a single place for all the groups (ie a railway station, a beach) only one set is necessary.

Concepts or attitudes

Consider the themes of friendship, loyalty, trust, happiness, loneliness, honesty, justice, thoughtlessness, carelessness, time, space, influence, pressure, pride, stubbornness, sexism, racism, etc. The exploration of abstract ideas can lead into abstract drama which often gives the opportunity for good use of space and movement.

Social issues

Consider the themes of leisure, famine, poverty or crime. These themes will need back-up information. Perhaps look at one aspect or storyline.

Humanity projects

For example, the Jarrow March, open-cast mining, ecology. Look at ideas that give the opportunity to create interesting conflicts. Through whose eyes is the story told? Would it be interesting to present different points of view? It is not necessary to tell the whole story of the Jarrow March.

Specific groups

Examine the different types of characters in particular groups, for example, police, teachers, doctors. Be careful not to stereotype.

Individual stories

Devise a situation that brings a group of people together, for example, a reunion. The drama could look at extracts from each person's life.

Page 70 can be used to jot down any ideas you would like to explore.

Exploring a theme

Either your teacher will set up some exploration sessions based upon a particular theme for all students to follow or, if students have chosen different themes, use a few sessions to explore their ideas. Consider genre as a way in which the same stimulus can be presented differently. Consider comedy, mime, soap opera, documentary, dramatic rhyme, a narrator or abstract form. If the idea is not working, do not be afraid to change it.

Choosing a group

Your teacher and your group need to consider who will benefit by working together, for example:

*   Will you benefit by working in a group with your friends?
*   Would it be better to work in a group that has a mixture of boys and girls, or in a single sex group?
*   Is everybody in the group reliable? If not, how can you encourage them to take the work seriously?

Once the themes are decided, make sure you know the examination requirements, as appropriate:

*   preparation time allowed
*   number of students per group
*   performance time
*   times and dates of final rehearsals
*   times and dates of the examination.

Complete these requirements on page 71. The presentations may be performed for an examiner but you may also want to invite an audience and devise your work for a target group.

Focus and title

Early on in the process you should choose a working title for your dramatic piece. Write down the content of the piece in one sentence. This should help you to choose a title. Is there a subtext? Can you write that in a sentence? For example:

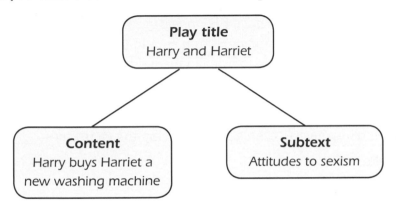

The diagram gives a focus. Filling in these boxes helps kick-start the process. It does not matter if the boxes are different at the end of the process. Use page 72 to help you.

Initial development of content

Draw up a scene synopsis (use page 74; an example is given on page 73). This will help with the direction of the piece. Once the general outline is established, you can begin the shaping of the improvisation. The whole process can take a long time. It is therefore important to keep motivated. As well as further discussions, the use of drama strategies and techniques will help you to shape the improvisation.

Members of your group or your teacher will suggest information and drama strategies at appropriate times. It may be possible for the teacher to suggest to all groups that they look at a particular drama technique at the same time. For example, early on in the preparation all students or groups could begin with a role-on-the-wall.

Shaping and character development

It is important to ensure that the characters you are portraying have credibility and interest for the audience. Even if the piece becomes very abstract in style, information derived from character work will be important to the development of the improvisation.

The entrance of a character is important. It establishes their role for the examiner or audience. You should think about the walk of the character, gestures that make them different to other characters, and ways of sharing thoughts, eg through reactions or directly addressing an audience.

The following are techniques to develop the character:

- Role-on-the-wall
- Switching roles
- Freeze-framing or thought in the head
- Hotseating or interviewing
- Creating scenes outside the drama or offstage life
- Re-enactment
- Forum theatre
- Character summary

These techniques not only help you to flesh out the character but can generate ideas for further plot development. More detail on these techniques can be found in *Chapter 3*. Further examples of points to consider when developing a character are as follows:

Movements
- What motivates a character's movement?
- Do they move slowly when they are tired?
- How do they move when they are angry?

Gestures

Body language can
indicate a person's
attitude. Closed gestures,
arms folded, can
visually confirm 'I'm not
interested'. Sometimes
communication can be
as simple as eye contact.
Try and develop for
a character particular
mannerisms that
set them apart from
other characters.

Language

Accents can be difficult to imitate and can lead to stereotyping.
The right register is more important than colloquialism. How a
person speaks is affected by how they are feeling at that moment
– nervous, happy, and so on.

During the early stages of improvisation, for example, you may find
that you 'pick up' on the previous spoken line; it gives you time to
think on the spot. Sometimes this creates unnecessary repetition.
However, the speech patterns can be developed creatively in a
positive way.

People have their own way of speaking. In these patterns they often
use particular phrases. Try to personalise the character's language.

Attitude and intention

What are the character's fears, hopes, needs? These all affect
movement, gesture and language. Know what the character
is thinking.

Pages 75 to 84 can be used to help you to make notes on
your character:

- Page 77 can be used to make basic notes about your character.
  Perhaps you could note six important facts about your character.
  Some example notes are given on page 76.

- Page 79 can be used to note any information you need to research. An example is given on page 78.
- Page 80 shows how you can record a character summary.
- Pages 83 and 84 are for you to make notes on the movements, gestures, language, attitude and intention of your character. If you try to explain the reactions of a character, for example, why they fold their arms, then this analysis can be useful to include in any written work that needs to accompany the practical work. Pages 81 and 82 offer an example.

These pages will help you to identify the development of your work when you look back over the process. Never leave the written work to the end of the practical process. Make notes and write down the changes you make as you create and rehearse the piece.

Developing the structure

Highlighting

Highlights can be used to deal with a section or the whole piece. A graph can show the frequency and degree of dramatic highlights.

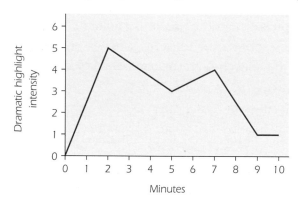

Imagine the diagram above charts a ten-minute improvisation. The first major highlight occurs after two minutes – this might be someone screaming, or running around frantically. From the second minute to the fifth minute the drama is calmer. After the fifth minute, tension begins to build up again, and falls off sharply after the seventh minute. This could be when an argument stops. Until the end of the improvisation there are no more real highlights.

The drama almost seems to fade away. If all the highlights occur at the beginning and middle of a drama, or worse, only at the beginning, then the audience will lose interest. If there are no real highlights, then the piece will be lacking in dramatic tension.

Consider these structuring suggestions:
- Would a change of mood benefit the piece?
- Are you clear about the beginning, middle and end of the piece?
- Can the piece be restructured to move particular highlights?
- Can other highlights be added to the piece?
- Is there a highlight at the end of the piece?
- Are the highlights too close together?
- How could sound and light be used?
- How will the highlights link together?

Think about your improvisation. Can you draw a graph of its dramatic highlights? (Use page 85.) Seeing the highlights in graph form will tell you whether the structure of your improvisation is good, or whether it needs rethinking.

How many scenes?

Try not to present too many scenes, as this makes the storyline disjointed which works against the building of dramatic tension. Think carefully about the use of blackout between scenes or sections – they are not always necessary. Sometimes a brief freeze and then simply walking to the next position can be more effective. Consider facing out of the drama – a character or a number of characters can simply turn out of the drama and face upstage. This cuts down intrusive stage traffic. For example, at the end of a scene you could hold a freeze-frame whilst the next part of the drama continues next to or around you. Using some of these techniques will create interesting visual effects and will show a greater knowledge of performance elements.

Getting the best from your voice

To help with the pace of your piece, try the following exercises:

Picking up cues

Pick a short extract from your presentation. With a partner, go over the dialogue, overlapping cues – this is where the first word of the next speaker's sentence overlaps the last word of the last speaker's sentence.

Pause

Choose another short extract of about six lines. Identify where pauses might be effective. For example, in the dialogue used below there may be a pause before the teacher's sentence, 'It's possible'.

> *Teacher:* The rehearsal begins at 5 o'clock.
>
> *Student:* Will it finish before six?
>
> *Teacher:* It's possible.

Clarity and pace

If the pace of the dialogue sounds right in the rehearsal then you are probably talking too fast. Try and listen to yourself as you speak. It will help to slow you down. Remember that the audience only gets to hear the line once. You could record extracts and listen to the clarity and the pace.

Volume

Check out if the performance can be clearly heard. Groups can help each other in this exercise by sitting where the audience would be. Listening as a member of the audience with eyes closed really helps focus on the volume of the piece. Do the actors use the full range of their voices?

Sound collage

Sound collage is a useful technique to add another dimension to part of the drama. Using voice overlap can build up tension, create pace and develop the drama into an abstract form. It adds interest to the drama and shows awareness of performance elements.

You may wish to make notes on page 87 on the results of these exercises. An example is given on page 86.

Costumes and key props

The use of costumes and props will help create the right mood and can confirm the period in which the improvisation is set. However, you do not want to be involved in numerous costume changes in a 20-minute improvisation. Consider the use of token costumes, eg using different hats, or something as simple as a scarf.

Any props you use should be really vital to the drama. If you are creating an improvisation, it is the characters and the plot that are important. If the improvisation is for an examination, then most examining boards have separate categories for design of costumes and props. In brief, keep everything simple and manageable.

Setting moods and establishing place

Music

Music selected for links should be reflective of past or future actions, and should underline the mood of the piece. If the presentation is only one short act then music at the beginning and ending helps set off the piece. Remember that the music should not impose too much. There should be no large sections of music with no drama taking place.

Sets

Very simplistic sets can often be as effective as elaborate ones. Simple colour backgrounds can give a unifying feel to a set of presentations. The colour(s) can also be symbolic of place or mood. For example, yellow for a beach, happiness or sunshine. The use of rostra and close lighting may be all that is needed.

Lights

Again, simplicity should be the principal consideration. The angles and intensity create different effects and, of course, the coloured gels will symbolise mood. However, remember that an examiner and the audience need to see. It is better to have too much light than not enough.

Design work

In any design work that accompanies your piece, you need to consider and make notes on the following:

- The atmosphere, meaning and style that the drama will convey. How can you contribute to this? For example, if it is set in the American Gangster era, or if it is futuristic, how could you show this? Would colour help, for example, what would blue lighting convey? How about red? Research can be very important at this stage, and careful notes should be made.

- Discuss the presentation with others in your group, and find out how they see it. Make notes of their requirements. Begin initial designs.

- Design lighting or sound plots, set, costumes and props in the context of the demands of the piece. Share the ideas with each other and note any comments. Make particularly sure that everything will be where it needs to be, and nothing will be in anyone's way. Record changes and developments.

- Construct the set, make costumes, hang lights, etc. Consider and record the differences between the design and the reality. What problems did you have, and how did you solve them?

- Discuss your ideas with the other actors. Have there been many changes? Consider the original concept. Is it still appropriate, and why?

- Record final designs.

- Consider what changes you need to make during the run. Note the details.

Cue sheets for sound and lighting are provided on pages 88 and 89.

Positions, sightlines and levels

The phrase 'blocking in' relates to the positions the actors take up in the acting area. The actors should be positioned so that they can be seen clearly by the audience. You and your teacher need to agree on the acting area and where the audience will sit. As an exercise, you could decide upon the most important or most exciting moment from your dramatic piece. Present a freeze-frame of the moment. Other students could comment briefly on the blocking. For example:

- Is the picture visually interesting?
- Are there improvements that could be made?
- Who is the most important person in the frozen picture?
- Are they in the most appropriate place?
- What is the picture saying?

Check the sightlines by asking other students to sit around the room.

Different levels can be used to emphasise status as well as creating visual images. Using characters from your dramatic piece, make a freeze-frame that shows at a glance the status of the characters in relation to each other. (See the cartoons of blocking in on page 38.) Try to use a variety of levels and bear in mind that status has a lot to do with how the character feels.

Space in the acting area can confirm the dramatic story visually. For example, if the piece concerns a conflict between a teenager and their family, the family could be grouped together and the teenager isolated to the left or right.

Use page 91 to make notes on positions, sightlines, levels, music, set, lighting and highlights. An example is given on page 90.

Rehearsals and performance

The final rehearsals are to polish the improvisation ready for performance. In the final stages it is wise not to add any new ideas. Concentrate on sorting out any technical problems, and becoming really confident with your piece. If the piece is to be presented to an examiner, it is a good idea to try it out in front of a small audience first. Perhaps invite a Year 7 class. The more performances you do, the more confident with the piece you will become.

Technical rehearsals

The aim during a technical rehearsal is simply to go from the beginning of the whole presentation right through to the end, checking scene links, music and sound cues. The majority of the dialogue, apart from cues, is omitted. You may find it difficult to get on with any other work, since it is a case of being ready when needed. Those responsible for lighting, sound and stage management should have all cue sheets prepared.

Technical rehearsals are a collective process and help to set the atmosphere of serious endeavour that will give confidence to everyone's performance. Establishing routines and responsibilities will lead to everyone having the calm competence from which artistic flair can grow.

Full rehearsal

Your aims here are to:

- go through the whole piece and hopefully get it right
- keep going even if something does go wrong
- check and note any details that need sorting out
- try and get the right pace and tempo in the piece
- consider how the audience will react (remember if an audience laughs, then you will have to briefly hold back the next line)
- put together the ingredients of the performance – acting, lighting, sound, costumes, props, etc.

Performance tips

If you are presenting an improvisation for another class or an examiner, you may need to be ready in the acting area. If this is the case, create a good impression by being still and calm. This will help you with your concentration. The examiner will look at how you are positioned before the drama begins – it sends out signals to them. Make sure you send the right signals.

Fidgeting

Try not to:

- flick your hair
- scratch
- rock on your feet
- keep turning round when facing out of the drama.

If it really becomes necessary to flick your hair out of your eyes, then try to do it in character. Then sort your hair so it is in place for the next performance.

Acknowledging others in the acting area

When you pass another character in the acting area during a performance, consider how you should react as you pass them. Does your character know them? Do you nod, smile, ignore them, etc?

Mistakes

If you make a mistake, don't laugh – that will make two mistakes! Try to continue as if nothing has gone wrong.

Blocking in

When presenting improvisations, always try to block in the actors downstage. It makes it easier for the audience to see and hear.

The use of the downstage area is very important. Consider key moments in an improvisation. Would you block them upstage or downstage? Using a small downstage area for the whole improvisation can create some interesting visual work. If you just use an area four metres by four metres, you are forced to use other techniques to create interesting visual images. For example, instead of exiting, the characters could just face out of the drama or hold a freeze-frame. This creates interesting drama and gives you the opportunity to show your understanding of various techniques.

Creating interesting pictures for the audience is important. The play is not a radio play but a play with words and visual action. In cinema, the director would be at pains to ensure that what we see is pleasing, atmospheric and appropriate.

Most people will be aware that the actors should not speak with their back to the audience, although occasionally breaking this 'rule' can create a dramatic effect. However, the majority of the time it is easier for the audience if they can see the actor clearly. Whenever possible, try to face the audience, keeping your shoulders towards them.

If you are using chairs, then set them at 45 degrees – again, this makes it easier for the audience to see.

Using upstage hand

Also consider the use of hands across the face. In the first picture below, actor A calls to actor B but covers his face with his downstage hand. This can muffle the sound of the voice and hides the facial expression from the audience.

In this picture, actor A uses his upstage hand which makes everything clearer.

On the day

Check all props, costumes, lights and sound. The audience and examiner have only one opportunity to understand all the thinking and creating that has been done over a number of weeks.

Special tips include:

- be ready
- speak so that the audience can hear and understand
- support one another in role, especially if mistakes are made
- it is too late to make any changes
- enjoy the performance
- organise clearing away for the next group.

Complete page 92 so that you have all the necessary information in one place. You may need to comment on the audience's reaction for your written coursework. If so, make brief notes as soon as possible on page 94 so that you do not forget. An example is given on page 93.

Preparing a dramatic piece for examination

In GCE A-level Performing Arts and all GCSE Drama courses there is the opportunity to develop a piece of drama from improvisation to a rehearsed presentation. You may have had this experience at Key Stage 3 as well.

A drama examiner looks for the following:
- spatial awareness, movement, gesture
- vocal quality, clarity, fluency, projection
- awareness of audience, awareness of performance elements, integration, communication
- control, appropriateness, conviction, credibility, support
- pace, timing
- interpretation, sustaining roles, responding.

These points can be placed under four headings:
1 Vocal quality
2 Supportive sustained role(s)
3 Use of space and movement
4 Performance elements.

The following tick boxes are to help you check individuals or a whole group. You can work with the people in your own group or with another group.

Vocal quality

	Yes	No
• Is the language used by the character appropriate?	☐	☐
• Does the language help to make the role credible?	☐	☐
• Can the vocals be heard?	☐	☐
• Are the vocals projected well to the audience?	☐	☐
• Are the vocals clear?	☐	☐
• Does the speaker show a clear understanding of what is being said?	☐	☐
• Is there rhythm, fluency and variation in the way the actors speak?	☐	☐

Supportive sustained role(s)

• Do the roles support and help the drama?	☐	☐
• Are the roles credible?	☐	☐
• Are the roles an important part of the drama?	☐	☐
• Are the responses to the action and dialogue believable?	☐	☐
• Do the actors concentrate and stay in role?	☐	☐

Use of space and movement

• Is the movement appropriate for the role?	☐	☐
• Is the blocking in for sightlines correct? (Can everyone be seen when necessary?)	☐	☐
• Is there any symbolic use of space, movement and gesture?	☐	☐
• Is space used to create interesting visual images?	☐	☐
• Do the gestures and movements make the roles better?	☐	☐
• Is space and movement used with purpose and to help communicate the role to the audience?	☐	☐

Performance elements

- Does the piece flow easily? ☐ ☐
- Is the piece disjointed in any places? ☐ ☐
- Are there any unnecessary blackouts or stage traffic? ☐ ☐
- Does the piece have purpose? ☐ ☐
- Does the piece communicate to an audience? ☐ ☐
- Are there a number of drama techniques included which help the roles and meaning? ☐ ☐

If the piece has to be produced for a specific target audience, then you need to note any additional requirements. It may be aimed at a particular community or age group. For example, the piece may have to be on bullying and be of interest to Year 7 pupils.

Summary of tips for developing an improvisation for presentation

- If the idea is not working, change it. However, try to get the drama started as soon as possible.
- Make sure that all students in your group have an equal opportunity to show what they can do.
- Complete focus boxes.
- Complete a role-on-the-wall.
- Creating visual images is important (the play is not for radio).
- Think carefully about the credibility of the dialogue.
- Check sightlines carefully.
- The examiner will only see the performance once – make sure you speak clearly.
- Make a list of any props and costumes you need. Check that they are in the correct position for the performance.
- If you make a mistake during the performance, keep going – it may not be obvious to the examiner or the audience.
- Make sure you understand the requirements of the examination performance.
- Make sure you know the date and time of your performance.

Themes

Ideas to explore

1 ....

....

....

2 ....

....

....

3 ....

....

....

4 ....

....

....

5 ....

....

....

6 ....

....

....

Examination requirements

Preparation time allowed

....

Number of students per group

....

Length of performance time

....

Dates and times of final rehearsals

....

....

....

Dates and times of the examination performance

....

....

....

Other notes

....

....

....

....

....

....

Focus

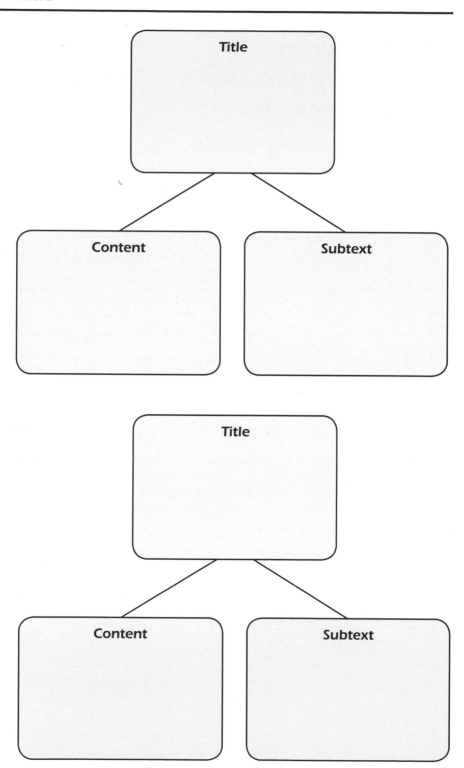

Synopsis sheet: Example

Improvisation synopsis

In the future all old people are 'taken away' at the age of 75.

Grandma's 75th birthday.

Characters

Grandma   Mary (Grandma's daughter)

Bill (Mary's husband)   Caitlin (grandchild)

Rebecca (grandchild)

Breakdown/scenes

Section 1   Family gets ready for the 'party'.

Section 2   Grandma arrives.

Section 3   Grandma remembers the good times.

Section 4   The van arrives to take Grandma away.

Section 5   The family say goodbye.

Section 6   Grandma leaves.

Synopsis sheet

Improvisation synopsis

....

....

Characters

....

....

....

....

Breakdown/scenes

Section 1   ....

....

Section 2   ....

....

Section 3   ....

....

Section 4   ....

....

Section 5   ....

....

Section 6   ....

....

Character description

Character notes: Example

Notes about my character(s)

1 Tom is 18 years old. He had never had a girlfriend.

2 He lives with his three sisters and mother.

3 His best friend is Sam.

   They are both interested in model railways.

4 He has done very well at school.

   He is expecting very good A-level results.

5 He has had a lot of trouble with another boy at school.

   The boy bullies Tom.

6 Tom likes Angela. She is 17 and lives round the corner.

Character notes

Notes about my character(s)

1 ....
....
....
....

2 ....
....
....
....

3 ....
....
....
....

4 ....
....
....
....

5 ....
....
....
....

6 ....
....
....
....

Character information to research: Example

Information about my character(s)

1   Some information about Tom's A-level courses

    – Geology and Spanish.

    ....

    ....

2   Names of makes of model trains.

    ....

    ....

    ....

3   Find out Spanish for 'How are you?' and

    'Will you go for a walk with me?'.

    ....

    ....

4   Find pictures of model trains.

    ....

    ....

    ....

5   ....

    ....

    ....

    ....

6   ....

    ....

    ....

    ....

Character information to research

Information about my character(s)

1 ....
....
....
....

2 ....
....
....
....

3 ....
....
....
....

4 ....
....
....
....

5 ....
....
....

6 ....
....
....
....

Character summary

One word or sentence that summarises my character

eg Thoughtful
....

....

....

....

....

....

One gesture that is frequently used or suggests my character

eg Rubs chin
....

....

....

....

....

....

One symbol that suggests or depicts my character

eg Arms folded moving to cupping face with hands
....

....

....

....

....

Character details: Example

Movement

I need to include some movements that suggest Tom is nervous
when speaking to Angela. In the scene when he sits next to her,
he should sit down very slowly.

Gestures

The constant rubbing of his chin with his thumb and index finger
suggests both his thoughtfulness and nervousness.

Language

He is confident when he speaks Spanish. I will have him speaking
some Spanish to Angela. There is some research to do on certain
Spanish expressions.

Attitude and intention

I need to show that he is interested in Angela in the first scene.

I will make him glance across at Angela several times.

Changes I have made to my role

During the scene when Tom asks Angela out his actions were too

nervous. They became comical. I have decided to make him

less nervous.

Reasons for the change

I want Tom to be less nervous because I want the audience to

always be on his side. When he was very nervous he became

comical and the audience were laughing at him.

Character details

Movement

....

....

....

....

....

....

Gestures

....

....

....

....

....

....

Language

....

....

....

....

....

....

Attitude and intention

....

....

....

....

....

....

Changes I have made to my role

....

....

....

....

....

....

Reasons for the change

....

....

....

....

....

....

Dramatic highlights

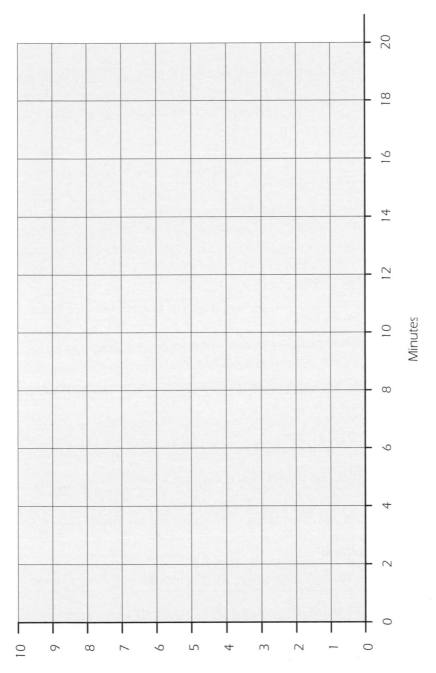

Dramatic highlight intensity

Minutes

Getting the best from your voice: Example

Picking up cues

I need to rehearse the scene between Tom and his best friend.

The dialogue is quite boring so we need to pick up the cues quickly.

Pause

When Tom asks Angela out, I need to pause briefly before asking.

Clarity and pace

During the bullying scene we need to speak more clearly. When

Tom defends himself the dialogue here should be said quickly.

Volume

I need to speak louder during the final date scene with Angela.

I have created the right tone but it is too quiet.

Sound collage

During the dream sequence we need to include a lot more different

expressions. Perhaps we should try to create about ten each.

Getting the best from your voice

Picking up cues

....

....

....

Pause

....

....

....

Clarity and pace

....

....

....

Volume

....

....

....

Sound collage

....

....

....

Cue sheet: Sound

Title of improvisation

....

Cue 1:
....

....

Cue 2:
....

....

Cue 3:
....

....

Cue 4:
....

....

Cue 5:
....

....

Cue 6:
....

....

Cue 7:
....

....

Cue 8:
....

....

Cue 9:
....

....

Cue sheet: Lighting

Title of improvisation

....

Cue 1: ....

....

Cue 2: ....

....

Cue 3: ....

....

Cue 4: ....

....

Cue 5: ....

....

Cue 6: ....

....

Cue 7: ....

....

Cue 8: ....

....

Cue 9: ....

....

Notes on dramatic piece: Example

Positions, sightlines, levels and use of space

It would be useful to create a level and leave it upstage centre.

This level can be used for the bully and Tom when he celebrates

his victory.

Music

The music used during the dream sequence is too loud. Perhaps we

should consider removing the music for this scene.

Set

The set can be symbolic. Against the back curtain we will hang

large cut-outs of Spanish expressions, model trains and

examination papers.

Lighting

We need blue lights during the dream sequence.

Highlights

The first bullying scene needs to be moved to halfway through the

improvisations. This will help with the balance of the highlights at

the beginning and end.

Notes on dramatic piece

Positions, sightlines, levels and use of space

....

....

....

Music

....

....

....

Set

....

....

....

Lighting

....

....

....

Highlights

....

....

....

Rehearsed presentation

Title of piece

....

Specific requirements

....

....

....

....

Actors and roles

....

....

....

....

....

....

Equipment, costumes and props

....

....

....

....

Day, date and time

....

Audience reaction: Example

- Was the content appropriate for the audience?
- Do you think the audience understood the content?
- Did the audience laugh or indicate emotional involvement in any other way, eg leaning forward at tense parts, responding to audience participation opportunities?
- Did presenting to an audience make any difference to the performance?

Write your immediate comments here

During our presentation I noticed that we all spoke a lot faster.

I think some of this was due to nerves. We all seemed to

concentrate better and picked up our cues quickly. This meant

that parts which had been slow in rehearsal, for example,

the 'snow scene', went a lot quicker.

During the scene when 'Mark' is hurt, there were a few gasps

from the audience. I think this helped us realise how effective

our drama was. This helped our confidence.

Audience reaction

- Was the content appropriate for the audience?
- Do you think the audience understood the content?
- Did the audience laugh or indicate emotional involvement in any other way, eg leaning forward at tense parts, responding to audience participation opportunities?
- Did presenting to an audience make any difference to the performance?

Write your immediate comments here

....

....

....

....

....

....

....

....

....

....

....

....

....

....

5 Producing written work

You will probably enjoy the practical side of drama, but may look upon the written work as a chore. A number of exam boards have tried to reduce the amount of written work required, however some still needs to be recorded.

Your written work celebrates your creativity. Try to regard it as a way of telling someone what you have learned through drama and what you have enjoyed about your work. The written work will help you to clarify your thinking about the drama process.

The written work is generally based on three aspects of the practical work:

- a series of improvisation lessons
- your development and presentation of a piece of drama
- appraisals and reviews of productions seen.

Within the development and presentation of a piece of drama, you may elect to concentrate on the technical side. For example, you may work on lighting, sound, costumes, properties, etc.

For any piece of written work at examination level, marks will be awarded for how analytical your work is – in other words, how you have evaluated the process. Note details of the drama form (the methods used) but do not just say what you did – explain why you did things in a certain way and which ways worked best.

Do not just be narrative – support the statements you make with evidence from your drama work. After each statement you write, ask yourself why or how. For example, 'I thought the drama was effective':

- Why?
- How?
- What was happening in the drama that made it effective?

Do not be tempted to leave the written work to the end of the project. After a period of several weeks, you will have forgotten parts of the lessons. It is wise to make simple notes as a project takes place. The notes give you some sort of record and note your reaction to the work. Sometimes your opinions will change as the work progresses. Without written notes you may forget parts of the development of the drama and your own responses. You can also make notes on:

- which techniques you used
- how the techniques were used
- how effective the techniques were
- which ideas worked, which did not and why
- thoughts for possible ways forward.

To note five points after each lesson takes very little time but the running record will prove very useful. For example, if you are writing up a unit of work for Key Stage 4 at the end of the project. Page 115 can be used for keeping brief notes. You may find the example sheet on page 114 helpful.

Tips

- Title your work clearly.
  - Write down the project title, eg loyalty.
  - Note the type of drama, eg improvisation.
  - Date the work.
- Keep working notes. Make notes on the drama work as the project goes along. Do not wait until the end to write your notes.
- Do not just be narrative. Support the statements you make with evidence from the drama.
- Use the vocabulary of drama when you can.
- Note what has interested you about the drama work.
- Try to state what you have learned through the drama.
- Try to remember if there were any particularly effective moments during the project. What was so effective about them, and why?
- Are there other drama techniques you think could have been included in the project? How would you have used them?

Pages 116 and 117 can be used to keep a record of your coursework. There is a column to add grades or marks for each piece of work.

Writing about improvisation

When writing a unit of work on a series of improvisation lessons, begin by considering the content or issues raised and think about the drama skills and techniques used.

Try to write in one or two lines what the topic is about.
For example:

> The topic was about stress and the different ways it affects people.

You can begin by stating what the topic is about and you could make some statement about what you have learned. For example:

> Our topic was about loyalty. It has brought to my attention the fact that being loyal does not necessarily always mean being completely honest.

You should then go on and explain how the drama work has made you draw such a conclusion.

Think about the drama skills and techniques used in the project. You may wish to list them as a reference to remind you as you write up your unit. The main technique used will probably be role-play. Be aware of how any techniques used in the role-play have contributed to your understanding of the content and credibility of the drama. For example:

> In my role-play I played a pregnant teenager about to tell her mother about the situation. In the role-play I did not tell my mother straight away – I kept asking her questions about teenage pregnancy. I did this to test how she might react when I told her about my situation. To me, this seemed a realistic way of tackling the situation. As I was asking the questions, I was leaving long pauses between each one. This allowed me to prepare what I was going to say next and helped build up the worries my character might be experiencing. The pauses also created an intense atmosphere helping both of us to become involved in the situation. This piece of drama helped me to realise how important silence is in creating atmosphere.

········

Jean had to walk through the thought tunnel and everyone had to call out how they thought Jean would be feeling as she walked to the social services. This gave us all a wider insight into her. Someone mentioned Jean's guilt. I hadn't thought that Jean could feel guilty so the thought tunnel made me think a bit more. It was also a good exercise for confidence and thinking quickly. During some pair work, I used the idea of guilt when I played Jean's father.

Note how other people's and the teacher's role-play can affect atmosphere and your own involvement.

In the short role-play I played Isobella, William's wife. I visited him in jail. Our teacher was in role as the jailer walking round, repeatedly saying 'Only a few minutes left and remember there is to be no physical contact'. This created a tense and daunting atmosphere, just knowing there was only a short time to say goodbye to your husband before he was killed. You weren't allowed to kiss or hug him one last time.

We sat facing each other and we both looked into each other's eyes. I felt extremely sad here. As the jailer made his way round telling us it was time to go, we stood up and I said 'I love you'. As I walked slowly past him, I instinctively shut my eyes and inhaled deeply, as if to get one last smell of him.

· · · · · · · ·

In the role-play I was the new manager of the supermarket. Everyone had worked there for a long time and they had all hoped that Peter would be the new manager. I decided to have a meeting with the staff. I felt very nervous before addressing them. I gathered them around me but everyone gave me a cold look. The cold look made me realise that the meeting was going to be difficult.

Writing about the language you or others have used in your role-play gives good evidence of your understanding of the content and the drama skills. For example:

> When I was in role as a miner, some of the language I used was not appropriate. For example, the time was 1832 but when I was addressing the other miners about the owners of the mine I used a modern expression: 'We're being ripped off'.

You can discuss aspects of the body language you use in your drama, for example:

> Andrew played the child. He sat slumped in the chair with his arms folded and refused to look at his parents. We decided Andrew should sit this way because we wanted to show he was unhappy.

········

> I showed my disappointment by walking slowly with my head down.

········

> When I went in, I waited for them to tell me to sit down. This would indicate to the audience that I was trying to be polite. I sat down with my back straight, crossed my legs and put my hands on my knees to show I was trying to make a good impression.

········

> At the beginning of the improvisation I was sitting down, but as time progressed and the stress built up I stood up to show I was angry. I also put my hand on my head to show I was upset. I turned away from my mum to show I was upset with her.

In the next example, a student comments on how her body language changed during the role-play:

> I walked over boldly to show that my character was annoyed. I wasn't feeling strong, just trying to appear so. When I confronted him my whole body language changed. At one time I even stepped back. I stuttered, I mumbled and kept repeating myself. I twiddled my fingers and kicked my feet. My partner realised he had the upper hand and acted as if he couldn't care. The role-play was spoiled when my partner pushed me as he walked away from me. I felt this was inappropriate.

Often your teacher will create situations where you will write in role. Writing in role shows how you understand the situation. It is a good idea to include extracts of your writing in role with some analysis. For example:

> *Dear Cath*
>
> *The trenches are cold, wet and dreary. We will be going over the top in one hour. See you when I get back.*
>
> *Love Bill.*

This is a piece of writing I completed when we were being soldiers in the trenches. Now that I have had time to consider it, I think it is not very realistic. It is too short and lacking any emotion. If someone was going over the top, there is the chance that they may be killed. Perhaps they would write a longer and more meaningful letter.

······

Diary extract:

> *William was taken to Durham jail last night. I will see him on Thursday. How will I pass these two days? The children have been taunted by other children in our street. Their dad's not a murderer. William is innocent but I don't believe he will be set free. They will hang him. No one has the right to do that. How strong will I be on that day? What will I do with the children? I'll have to be there. I don't want to go. I won't be able to look at him but he'll need me there. Maybe he shouldn't see me. I don't know what to do. I think, I write, I pray but there's never any sort of answer.*

This is an extract from my diary when I was playing Isobella Jobling in the role-play. It was written three hours (drama time) after I was given the news that William would be hanged on Saturday. As Isobella, my minded hopped from thought to thought: thinking about William, thinking about how I would cope, and thinking about the children. I think the work is effective and shows my understanding of my role. Maybe the diary writing might have been a little more emotional.

As you create improvisation work, you will make decisions. Try to note them and, more importantly, state why you made them. For example:

> We decided to put together two scenes showing a poor family and a rich family. We chose breakfast as the time for both as it showed both families in typical everyday situations and the contrast between the two could be emphasised.

· · · · · · · ·

> The drama needed to end with the witches vanishing. To symbolise this, we had them returning to a lower level and curling up. We also thought it was a good idea to end the drama with Macbeth on a higher level than Banquo as he had more status at that moment.

· · · · · · · ·

> We had the two children standing in the same position alongside each other to represent the equality that should have existed between them. We placed the teacher slightly forward of the children to show that she was in charge and was leading them.

· · · · · · · ·

> The first part of the improvisation showed us standing in a line. This showed the audience that we were all equal – nobody had higher or lower status. Katie ran on and we began to circle her. Katie slowly curled herself up in a ball. This showed her as the victim and her fear.

· · · · · · · ·

> There was a lot of silence to show that it would be a really awkward situation to be in. It would create a tense atmosphere so that the audience would not know who was going to speak next.

· · · · · · · ·

> The way we acted towards each other changed between scenes a lot. When we were happy, we had contact with each other. We made sure we were all touching in some way. This showed that we were all working together and bonding. When we wanted to show that we had fallen out, we made sure there was no contact. Everyone stayed in their own space onstage.

· · · · · · · ·

As we walked away from the bus stop, my friend turned her head and looked at the baby. We then froze, showing how much regret we had. We also thought that both the girls would want to have one last look at the baby and would want to keep the image in their heads. I think that this simple presentation was very effective because there was very little speaking throughout.

••••••••

The drum was tapped throughout and symbolised the heartbeat of us, the victims. Towards the end of the improvisation, we all knelt on the floor and repeated the word 'die'. We whispered it. The drumbeat became quieter and quieter until it stopped. The stopping of the drumbeat symbolised our death. Our heads were down and the audience was silent.

You can also state what might have been a better idea:

On reflection, the final freeze-frame could have been more symbolic if I had held an empty beer glass upside down. This would have indicated that money for the business had run out.

••••••••

The breakfast scene made its point, but maybe we could have created two further brief scenes to emphasise the differences between the families. Perhaps someone receiving a gift, or someone buying some clothes.

••••••••

The scene with the witches could have been improved by using slow motion as the witches curled up.

Writing about your prepared presentation

There are two main considerations when writing about your prepared presentation:

- The development – how the ideas have been formulated and what changes have been made to the piece throughout the rehearsals.
- The presentation – the performance.

It is probable that each time you run through either part or all of the improvisation, you will make changes or small adjustments. These need to be noted so that at the end of the project these notes can be written up into your unit of work.

With a good set of working notes you should be able to evaluate the process well and make precise references to the development of the drama.

How you use space is important and there are often changes to make here. You may make changes to the blocking. Blocking is how the actors are positioned in the acting area:

- You may make adjustments so that the actors can be seen clearly by the audience.
- You may decide that someone needs to move further up or downstage so that when someone crosses from left to right they do not have to walk round someone. Keeping the stage traffic flowing easily helps with the pace and overall effect of the piece.
- The blocking may symbolise something.

If you note this in your written work and justify your reasons, this is good analytical work. For example:

> We placed John centre stage for the second scene because he was the main character of the story. We did not move John. We wanted the other characters to come to him. In a way, this showed he had some sort of power over them. As he was in the centre we could bring characters on from both sides of the stage thus avoiding any problems of people on the stage being in anyone else's way.

If the actors continually make exits and entrances this can spoil the flow of the piece. You can comment on different techniques you have used. As you justify them, this is again good analysis. For example:

> In our short piece of drama, each of us played three characters. In order to save time and too much unnecessary movement in the acting area, each time we changed character we would move upstage and face out of the drama thus indicating to the audience that the character was not in the drama. As we took on our next role, we simply turned into the drama.

·········

> Our brief improvisation showed the thoughts a teenager was having about his mother and father constantly arguing. At first, we had a brief scene with the mother and father arguing, then they would exit. Their son would enter and talk directly to the audience about the problem with his mother and father. I liked the idea of the teenager talking to the audience but we needed to make it more effective. We did this by keeping the parents on stage and getting them to hold a freeze at a particular point in their argument. The teenager entered and moving from stage left to stage right as he spoke he could point at the freeze and talk about his parents to the audience. I felt this had more impact because there was a picture there always reminding the audience of the problem. We decided that after the teenager spoke he would exit, then his parents would begin arguing again.

You will make changes to the characters you create by using drama techniques to develop the character. For example, you may use the role-on-the-wall technique to make up further information. You may use thought in the head, freeze-frame, hotseating or create a scene that involves your character before the main drama story begins. Explain the techniques you use and how they helped you develop character. Being able to use drama terms correctly is important in the written work.

You may want to comment on how you used dialogue or voice patterns so that it could have the correct emotional impact. For example:

> When I was in role I spoke quietly and slowly to show I was worried about telling Tom I was going to leave him.

••••••••

> In our drama I played a girl who was leaving her boyfriend. At first, when we practised the scene, we both did a lot of shouting. In order to give contrast to the noise of the argument, before I left I decided to whisper my last line aggressively. This created a better dramatic impact because of the contrast and it seemed to force the audience to listen carefully to what I felt was the most important line.

••••••••

> In my role, I eventually knelt down and put the baby on the ground. We very slowly stood up to show how hard it was to say goodbye. My friend looked at the baby and then at me. I looked at the baby and said, 'I hope you can forgive me'. I think the simplicity of this line made the audience think about what was happening and would make them feel more involved.

If your drama is more abstract in form you may analyse particular use of words. For example:

> We created a poem to explain to the audience about a baby who had been abandoned. We described the baby as 'defenceless'. We thought that this word let the audience know how weak the baby was. Claire placed the baby centre stage so it would be the main focus for the audience. At the end of the poem we stood still, lifted our heads and whispered to the audience the word 'Helplessness'. We repeated it over and over, eventually fading it out. This was to symbolise that the baby could be dying. Hopefully, the silence at the end of the drama left the audience wondering what was going to happen to the baby.

> We used the word 'helpless' a lot as we thought it was important to let the audience know how weak the baby was, and how defenceless it was.

During the first presentation you need to consider if there is any difference between that performance and the final dress rehearsal. Note any developments that take place if the presentation is performed more than once. Consider what difference any audience makes to the performance. If it makes you more nervous, what difference does this make to the performance? For example:

> Sarah was nervous and spoke too quickly. Unfortunately, it was difficult for the audience to understand some of her dialogue. It was evident from the conversations afterwards with members of the audience that they had missed important parts of the plot.

Audience response is important and does need to be commented on. Consider the following:

- Did you have the audience sitting in a particular place? Why?
- Did you make any contact with the audience during the performance? Was it successful? Did you manage to keep in control?
- Did the age of the audience help you decide on the content and style of performance?
- Did you pitch it right?
- Did the audience respond as you thought they would?
- Do you think the audience understood what you wanted to say?

For example:

> As the lines were said, the group moved closer to the audience so they would feel intimidated and would think about what we were saying. As the line 'All the strangers passing by' was said, the outer people crossed by each other and walked past the middle person. This not only symbolised what was being said, but also allowed some movement as we had stood still for a long time. To finish, we all said the last line 'Why?' together. This made it louder and would make the audience think about why someone would abandon a baby. We said the word forcefully and with full eye contact with the audience.

•••••••••

At the end of our play we asked the audience to tell us words that we used in the play to describe how a victim feels. They told us 12 different words. I was pleased that they seemed to understand and remember the points we were making about the victim.

••••••••

Some of the jokes we presented were probably too babyish for Year 11. They did not laugh. In fact, in some parts a few people in the audience talked before the end of the joke. Obviously, they were losing interest in the improvisation.

Writing appraisals and reviews

An appraisal or review is a response to a play or production. The writer will consider how well the play was interpreted and performed. There are a number of professional critics who write for newspapers. Plays and productions are reviewed very early in their run; often there will be preview nights when newspaper critics are invited. A poor review could mean that the production may not become popular with the general public.

Always begin your review with the following details:
* name of the production
* name of the company performing the production
* name of the playwright
* place of performance
* date of performance.

As you write the appraisal, consider the type of company, eg professional or amateur, and the audience the performance is aimed at, eg teenagers or adults. This should affect your expectations. There is no need to note these with the details listed above as you will make reference to them in the appraisal.

It is not necessary to write a short paragraph on the storyline and background of the production unless your teacher specifically asks you to.

The more productions you see and the more you write about them, the better your appraisals will become. If your course only requires you to write about one production, it is still a good idea to see as many productions as you can.

Write about the production as soon as possible. Do not leave it for a week. Write down your immediate thoughts. Maybe note:
* what you considered to be the highlight
* what you will remember about the play and why
* what you would want to change and why
* whether it kept your attention all the way through
* what you felt about the overall standard.

A five-point appraisal sheet is provided on page 119. Complete it immediately after seeing a production. The five points need not necessarily be the same as the points mentioned on page 109. Simply note five points that strike you about the production. Use this as the basis for your appraisal. You may find the example on page 118 helpful.

Audience awareness

When you watch a production, look out for the ways in which the director has tried to ensure that the audience understands various points, does not miss out on important parts of the play and feels involved with the production. For example:

> As the play started with the prologue, the man stood on a box so the audience's attention would be directed towards him. He spoke very loudly, slowly and very clearly. I think this made the audience realise that this part of the play needed to be listened to very carefully.

········

> The actor playing Romeo sat in the audience and spoke his thoughts out loud. This made the audience feel more involved because it was as if he was talking to us.

You do not need to write about everything in the production. After your initial considerations, select some areas and write in detail. Always support any comment with direct references to the production seen. For example:

> I liked the performance of the actor who played Malvolio. He walked in a haughty way which suggested the personality of Malvolio. I have always felt that Malvolio does not have time for people. I liked the way the actor continually waved his right hand as if dismissing anyone he was talking to. This and many other gestures, for example, the lifting of his head when speaking to Sir Toby, contributed in creating the snobbishness of the character.

········

> The fairy's side of the stage was lit very brightly. This suggested to the audience that she was angelic and pure. On the other side of the stage was the horrible Sticksaw. His side of the stage was lit with greens to suggest the evilness of his character. Sound was

also used several times to create the same effect. When the fairy spoke, soft angelic music was played. When Sticksaw spoke, loud threatening music was played.

You should show that you understand the meaning of what the drama has communicated. Consider how the piece has done this. For example:

When I watched *Oh What a Lovely War*, I liked the way every time a soldier died one of the actors gave a member of the audience a poppy. The poppy symbolised the death and the giving of the poppy involved the audience in thinking about that death.

········

To show that Macbeth was frightened of what he was being told, he walked backwards away from the witches. This showed he did not trust the witches.

The use of symbolism is important and will often contribute greatly to the meaning of the play. It can often be seen through the costumes and lighting. For example:

Tony and Maria came from opposite sides of the stage and met in the centre. They moved slowly, contrasting with the quick energetic dancers onstage. As they met, they began to dance, looking into each other's eyes, but the main symbolism was how they danced. When they put their hands towards each other, they did not make contact but always kept a small distance between them. To me, this symbolised that they were not allowed to be together and, as the story would show, they could never be together.

········

One of the actresses, who played a witch, stood on a higher level to show her dominance over Macbeth.

········

All the good soldiers were dressed in white and the evil landowners were dressed in black.

········

I think the director chose the colour red for the flag because red represents blood. There was a lot of red in this production to symbolise the blood. Another example was at the end of the battle when the stage was flooded with red light.

Consider exits and entrances, stage traffic and the links between scenes. These all contribute to the pace of the piece, for example:

In *Barnum*, I liked the way the actors juggled with the props and scenery for the following scene. It kept the whole production moving, it was entertaining, it was in-keeping with the circus theme, and it contributed to the overall pace of the production.

What sort of atmosphere was the director trying to create? For example:

The scene was supposed to be set in a lively tavern, however everyone on stage was very static and quiet. I think the scene needed some music to begin with and much more movement during the whole scene.

Look at the audience around you. How are they reacting? Where are they sat? Are the actors involving the audience in any way? For example:

There were five different entrances, all through the auditorium. The audience felt involved as the actors travelled through and played off them. For example, in a child's sword-fighting scene, the actors attacked the audience. This created a good fun start to the scene that later would involve a lot of audience participation.

Other things to bear in mind include:
• Was the storyline credible?
• Did this affect the style of the production in any way?
• What sort of atmosphere did the director create?
• Which parts of the production did you find the most interesting?
• Which parts did you find dull?
• Did you concentrate throughout the performance?
• If you were directing the performance, what changes would you make and why would you make them?
• What was the style of the presentation?

- What was effective or problematic with the stage traffic?
- Was the blocking in effective?
- How were the actors grouped?
- How was space used?
- Was any symbolism used?
- Did any of the performance involve the audience?
- Consider the actors' interpretations of the characters. Did you agree with them?
- Did the actors use any particular mannerisms for their characters?
- Why were the mannerisms effective or not?
- Was voice projection acceptable?
- Were voice patterns effective?
- How did the actors react to the other characters on stage?
- Did the actors concentrate?
- Were the actors aware of the audience?
- How did the actors use props?
- Were the links between scenes effective?
- Were any special effects used?
- How did the lighting and sound contribute to the atmosphere?
- Was the production clearly lit?
- Was music used to underscore or create effects, tension, etc?
- Was the music too loud or too quiet?
- Was the music appropriate?
- Was music used to link scenes?
- Were the costumes modern?
- Did the actors use token costumes?
- What did the costumes tell you about the characters?
- Were the colours of the costumes significant?
- Were the colours of the set symbolic?
- What type of set was it?
- Was it abstract or realistic?
- How much space was used?
- Were there any special features?

Page 120 can be used to list the performances you have seen and to note brief details about them.

Notes for written work: Example

Project title   Animal rights and wrongs

Date   July 2003

1   Pair work, group work, large group work – preparing freeze-frames.
Easier to work in small group. As groups become bigger, more
difficult to listen and organise.

2   Freeze-frame of eight people entering a circus. Brought to life.
Needs a loud cue to signal freeze. Used ringmaster saying
'Hurry along'.

3   Easy to block in freeze-frame but when brought to life many of us
had our backs to the audience. It was difficult to keep clear
blocking in with eight people.

4   Poor blocking in for final freeze-frame meant some of us
could not be seen when we addressed the audience with
our thoughts.

5   When we addressed the audience we could have stepped
forward thus stepping into view.

Notes for written work

Project title ....

Date ....

1 ....
....
....
....

2 ....
....
....
....

3 ....
....
....
....

4 ....
....
....
....

5 ....
....
....
....

Key Stage 3

Work set	Deadline	Completed
....	....	....
....	....	....
....	....	....
....	....	....
....	....	....
....	....	....
....	....	....
....	....	....
....	....	....
....	....	....
....	....	....
....	....	....
....	....	....
....	....	....
....	....	....
....	....	....
....	....	....
....	....	....
....	....	....
....	....	....

Key Stage 4

Title of topic	Deadline	Mark/Grade
....	....	....
....	....	....
....	....	....
....	....	....
....	....	....
....	....	....
....	....	....
....	....	....
....	....	....
....	....	....
....	....	....
....	....	....
....	....	....
....	....	....
....	....	....
....	....	....
....	....	....
....	....	....
....	....	....
....	....	....
....	....	....

Appraisal immediate thoughts: Example

Name of production   Bus shelter

Name of company   Tynemouth Tourers

Name of playwright   Kevin Wilson

Place of performance   Uppington School Drama Studio

Date of performance   January 2003

1   Lots of blue light used to suggest the coldness of December. Single spotlight on the abandoned baby emphasised the loneliness, etc.

2   Use of warm colours in lighting when baby reunited with her mother.

3   Speech of friend of mother not clear. Needed to speak slower.

4   The comic routine of the milkman was a welcome relief half-way through this sad story.

5   At times too much of the acting was upstage. The reunion should have been presented downstage.

Appraisal immediate thoughts

Name of production   ....

Name of company   ....

Name of playwright   ....

Place of performance   ....

Date of performance   ....

1   ....

....

....

2   ....

....

....

3   ....

....

....

4   ....

....

....

5   ....

....

....

Performances seen

Title	Company	Venue	Date
....	....	....	....
....	....	....	....
....	....	....	....
....	....	....	....
....	....	....	....
....	....	....	....
....	....	....	....
....	....	....	....
....	....	....	....
....	....	....	....
....	....	....	....
....	....	....	....
....	....	....	....
....	....	....	....
....	....	....	....
....	....	....	....
....	....	....	....
....	....	....	....
....	....	....	....
....	....	....	....

Useful words

This section lists words you will find useful when completing written work. You may also wish to add words of your own.

Abstract	Accompaniment	Acoustics	Acting area
Action	Actor	Actress	Aesthetic
Amplifier	Amplifying	Analogy	Analysis
Angle	Appear	Appraisal	Appreciate
Appropriate	Apron	Assistant stage manager	
Atmosphere	Attitude	Audible	Audibility
Audience	Auditorium		

Backcloth	Backstage	Barn door	Bass
Batten	Battery	Beginners	Beginning
Believable	Believe	Bias	Blackout
Blocking	Blocking in	Body language	Box office
Box set	Bringing to life	Budget	Bulb

Candle	Canvas	Carpenter	Caption
Cassette	Castors	CD	Centre
Changeover	Channel	Character	Characterisation
Choreographer	Chorus pedal	Cinemoid	Circle
Clarity	Colour	Comfort	Comedy
Comical	Commitment	Communication	Concentration
Confidence	Construction	Content	Control
Control desk	Copyright	Costume	Creative
Creativity	Credible	Credibility	Crew
Criticism	Cross over	Cue	Cut-out
Cyclorama			

Decision	Definite	Design	Designer
Development	Dialogue	Digital	Dimmer
Director	Discussion	Docudrama	Downstage
Drama	Dramatic	Drape	Dress rehearsal
Durability			

Echo	Effect	Effective	Electrician
Electricity	Emotion	End on	Engineer
Entrance	Equipment	Evaluate	Evaluation
Exaggerate	Exaggeration	Exercise	Exit
Experience	Expert	Expression	Extract

Fading	Feedback	Final	Finding your light
First night	Fitting	Fixed set	Flash button
Flat	Flood	Flying in	Focus
Foldback	Follow spot	Footwear	Form
Framing	Freeze-frame	Fresnel spotlight	Front of house
Fuse			

'G' clamp	Gain	Gesture	Giving witness
Gobo	Good/bad angel	Graphic equaliser	Ground plan
Group			

His/her thoughts	Hotseat	Houselights	Humorous
Image	Improvisation	Inaudible	Information
Integrated	Interviewing	In the round	Input
Issue	Instruments		
Jackplug	Jester		
Language	Lantern	Level	Lighting
Make-up	Mannerism	Mood	Motivate
Motivation	Movement		
Nervous			
Offstage	Onstage	Operate	Organise
Output			
Pan	Pantomime	Partner	Patching
Performance	Performance rights	Period	Permission
Photographer	Picture	Piece	Playwright
Plug	Point of view	Practical	Practice (noun)
Practise (verb)	Premiere	Prepare	Presence
Presentation	Promenade	Producer	Production
Professional	Profile spotlight	Programme	Promenade
Prompter	Properties	Proscenium	Public
performance	Publicity	Purpose	
Question			
Realistic	Recording	Re-enactment	Refreshments
Rehearsal	Rehearse	Represent	Reprographics
Reverb	Review	Role	Role-play
Role-on-the-wall	Rostra	Rostrum	Round
Royalty	Run	Runner	
Safety chain	Scene	Scenery	Score
Script	Secret role-play	Sensitivity	Sequencing
Set	Set design	Shadow	Shakespeare
Sightline	Situation	Snap blackout	Socket
Social	Soliloquy	Solo	Solo thinking
Sound	Sound effects	Speaker	Special
Split staging	Spotlight	Stage	Stage direction
Stage manager	Stage traffic	Staging	Status
Stereotype	Striking the set	Strobe lighting	Style
Success	Supervision	Sustain	Switch
Swivel set	Symbol	Symbolic	Symbolising
Symbolism			
Teacher-in-role	Technical	Technician	Technique
Telephone	Tension	Text	Theatre
Theatre in the round	Theme	Thought	Thought tunnel
Thrust	Ticket	Timer	Tone
Torch	Tragedy	Transmitter	Traverse
Treble	Turning through the audience		
Understudy	Uplighting	Upper deck	Upstage
Visual	Voice		
Wardrobe	Wings		